IMAGES OF ENGLAND

Wigston Magna and South

Mr Grundy, the Wigston stationmaster, around the end of the nineteenth and the beginning of the twentieth centuries.

IMAGES OF ENGLAND

Wigston Magna and South

Duncan Lucas, Tricia Berry
and Peter Mastin

NONSUCH

Advertising postcard, c. 1930. One of a series
of four advertising cards published by the Two
Steeples company, one of Wigston's largest
hosiery and knitwear manufacturers. The town
was often called 'Wigston-Two-Steeples', being
one of the very few places in England to have
two parish churches.

First published 1997
This new pocket edition 2006
Images unchanged from first edition

Nonsuch Publishing Limited
The Mill, Brimscombe Port,
Stroud, Gloucestershire, GL5 2QG
www.nonsuch-publishing.com

Nonsuch Publishing is an imprint of Tempus Publishing Group

British Library Cataloguing in Publication Data.
A catalogue record for this book is available from the British Library.

ISBN 1-84588-335-7

Typesetting and origination by Nonsuch Publishing Limited
Printed in Great Britain by Oaklands Book Services Limited

Contents

Acknowledgements

We would like to thank the numerous people who have, over the years, provided access to their personal collections of photographic and other material so that it may be shared with others. Also to Neville Chadwick, Wigston's own photographer, for often providing us with copies of borrowed material at no charge.

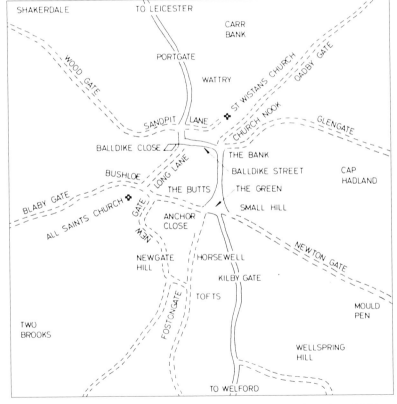

Map of Wigston Magna in the Middle Ages with the old names of roads, tracks and fields.

Introduction

The authors of this work would each like to record their feelings for their home town.

Despite the proximity of Leicester, Great Wigston has always been of an independent mind. Second in population in the county for many years, the town's background of not having any squires for centuries has left its mark. Many individuals owned land and property. When the Industrial Revolution arrived this meant that our township easily absorbed incoming families and the native families remained here.

To cater for the needs of industry much of our heritage in the form of buildings was destroyed, to make way for factories and the rows of cottages needed to house the servants of the machines. The ancient families stayed but the buildings did not. Be careful to whom you gossip in Old Wigston, most of the original families are related!

All of this makes it even more important to record what has gone before. The memories of people fade and much that is recorded in the captions of this book has been given orally. All three of the authors are avid recorders of Wigston's proud past. From the Iron Age to the Romans, the Saxons and Danes who settled here side by side at the beginning of the settlement and left us the legacy of two churches and two manors. Then the Normans came and recorded us in the Domesday Book. Only a few artefacts and documents plus the two ancient churches survive as records of those centuries. Then the camera was invented and from the 1850s we can see what some of the town and its people looked like.

As you turn the pages of this book you can step back in time. I am proud to be a part of this book for it records my own family as well as my town. My childhood scenes are there and if it gives you, dear reader, additional pride in our heritage then it was worth all the effort. If you would like to see more photographs we have a large number in the Wigston Folk Museum.

Duncan Lucas

Putting into words 'what Wigston means to me' has proved more difficult than I imagined. In a word I suppose it means home, a feeling of belonging, arising perhaps from the fact that I have lived nearly all my life in the area and heightened more recently by the discovery that three separate branches of my ancestors lived and worked within the parish for many generations.

My interest in the history of Wigston is a progression from the family history research I felt motivated to begin after the death of my much loved father and the consequent passing on to me of a family bible with various birth and death dates and a small collection of photographs. I suddenly realised that I knew very little of my father's early life and still less of the Wigston in which he grew up; this set me on a determined course of discovery. Fifteen years on I am still discovering and as immersed as ever in this fascinating hobby.

This interest led me to begin a collection of photographs, most of which were originally produced as postcards. They show a Wigston changed almost beyond recognition. The postcards were often commissioned and sold by local shopkeepers such as Primrose Wray, W.B. Roberts & Son, Shipps and G.N. Proctor, or as advertising cards such as the Two Steeples Jersey Girl and Durham Ox pub examples which are illustrated within. They might have been produced locally too. Hall's of South Wigston took many photographs which were used as postcards, as did T.E. Moore just over the Leicester boundary in Queens Road who often identified his work by the initials MCPL (Moore, Clarendon Park, Leicester) in the bottom right-hand corner. Many were then issued as photographic cards while others were printed and Deeming Brothers of South Wigston were responsible for quite a number.

My co-authors Duncan, Peter and I hope that these bygone treasures, which have been selected from our various collections, prove interesting. We would like to offer a grateful word of thanks to all those busy photographers who took the trouble to record the everyday scenes around them and to the previous owners who carefully preserved them, thus ensuring their survival into today's very different world.

Tricia Berry

Like my two fellow authors I was born to a Wigston family and I live here today. I am also the odd one out, for at the age of sixteen my family emigrated to the other side of the world and it was twenty-four years before I returned. They say that you do not really appreciate something until you no longer have it and that was certainly true for me. The familiar names and streets of my childhood were suddenly only memories and the occasional photograph in a book or newspaper forwarded by kindly relatives. Commitments to a family delayed my return, but the knowledge that I would one day do so was always there. I can still remember clearly my feelings as I first drove into Wigston again. So little had changed, so much that was familiar remained.

History has always interested me and steering that interest into my native town has revealed a tapestry of life far more intriguing than any best-selling novel. Wigston has no particular national claim to fame, yet in many ways it is a perfect microcosm of the history of England. When one discovers some new piece of historical information, suddenly other pieces already known fall into place and one's understanding of human history is further enriched. With the benefit of maturity I can appreciate the endeavours of my ancestors in laying the foundations of our modern life.

On my return to Wigston I discovered there was a thriving local history group. The Greater Wigston Historical Society made me very welcome and further fuelled my thirst for knowledge. Many of its members had their own specialised fields of interest and their combined pool of knowledge was vast. My particular interest was in Wigston's railways, for as a child I had spent countless hours on the Kop watching the endless procession of steam-hauled trains. This field led me to look at South Wigston which had two of the town's three stations. Other aspects of this nineteenth century 'new town' began to vie for my attention and now I seem to be specialising in that other part of Wigston 'over the bridge'. Although I have never lived near to Blaby Road, many of my family have and my parents were married at St Thomas' church. One day I will have recorded all that there is to record of South Wigston and will turn my attention again to 'top' Wigston to see what wants doing there!

It has been a privilege to be asked to co-edit this book with Tricia and Duncan and I would like to dedicate my share of it to all the kind people who have lent and given material freely over the years. Without them there would be no book, for none of the photographs were taken by the authors. If anyone has any material they think could be of interest in future volumes, please contact any of us. Anything lent will be copied and returned and you will have contributed to the record of your town's history.

Peter Mastin
January 1997

One

Before 1900

Wigston Station, *c.* 1899.

Above: South Wigston Wesleyan Chapel, c. 1895. This was the original frontage of 1886, set back from Blaby Road. The chapel was substantially extended in 1902 and this building was incorporated into the rear section of the new structure and is now used as a schoolroom. The two gentlemen are Mr H. Dougherty and Mr G. Dalton with Mrs Fitchett standing on the right.

Left: The Plough Inn, Bushloe End, c. 1896. The landlord at this time was Joseph Potter and the name of the inn most probably originates from the medieval practice of keeping the village plough in the nearby church. Today's Plough Inn stands on the same site although very little, if any, of the original structure remains. Beyond the pub can be seen the framework knitter's cottage and shop which today forms the Wigston Framework Knitting Museum. It is preserved in much the same condition as it would have been at the time of this photograph.

Life Boys parade in Blaby Road, *c.* 1899. The Life Boys were the forerunners of today's Boy's Brigade, a youth movement of the nonconformist churches. The Church of England equivalent were called Church Lads.

Bassett Street Infant's School, South Wigston. Class IV of 1895.

Blaby Road and Wigston Station, *c.* 1899. The station building dates from the opening of the Leicester to Hitchin line of the Midland Railway in 1857. Ten years later the railway was extended from Bedford to St Pancras and became the main line from Leicester to London. By the date of this photograph the heavy railway traffic caused frequent delays to road users on their way from Wigston to South Wigston and Blaby over the level crossing adjacent to the station. In 1900 work began on the construction of an overbridge on this site and this station was demolished to be replaced by a new station with most of its offices at road level on the bridge. The new structure opened in 1902 and became known as Spion Kop after a contemporary battle in the Boer War. The bridge still stands although the station closed in 1968 and was later pulled down. The houses behind the signal box are Midland Cottages and were built by the railway company to house some of its employees when the engine shed and wagon repair shops were opened in the 1870s. Beyond the level crossing gates can be seen the Railway Hotel (now the 1852), while houses are beginning to appear along Station Road. Nearly all of the houses seen here are still standing.

Wigston Station yard and road entrance, *c.* 1896.

Wigston Station, *c.* 1880. The locomotive is standing on the level crossing over Blaby Road and a comparison with the photograph on page 9 shows the signal box has been moved to the other side of the main line. With the construction of the road bridge the box was moved again, closer to Leicester.

Above: Walden's shop, *c.* 1895. This was situated on the first bend in Oadby Lane where Glebe Close now joins the road.

Left: Clark's Confectionary Shop, *c.* 1899. A long-standing Wigston name and a typical shop of the period. Many people entered the retail trade by converting the front room of their house into a small shop. Many failed but some prospered and expanded into some of today's well-known stores.

St Thomas' Church, South Wigston, c. 1899. Built in 1893, a tower was added in 1900 and was largely financed by Thomas Ingram, a prominent Wigston lawyer. The land for the church was given by Orson Wright although the building contract was awarded to Mr Bland who had submitted a lower tender than Mr Wright. The church and vicarage were designed by Stockdale Harrison and both are now listed buildings.

South Wigston Wesleyan Chapel Choir, c. 1896.

Mowsley End, c. 1899. The wall towards the top of the street surrounds the Chestnuts, a substantial private house.

Oadby Lane, c. 1898. This view is looking down towards the Bank and to the left is Church Nook with the wall of St Wolstan's House beneath the trees. This wall still stands but every other building in this picture has been swept away with the development of the modern dual carriageway. Although long since renamed Oadby Road, one still hears the older residents of Wigston refer to the wide modern road as Oadby Lane.

Above: Staff at Wigston Station, March 1900.

Right: The Dougherty family of South Wigston, *c.* 1895. Mr Dougherty was a goods guard on the Midland Railway and a staunch member of the Wesleyan chapel. The children are, from left to right: Will, Grace, Nellie and Annie. The two elder daughters can be identified in the photograph of the Wesleyan choir on page 15.

Crow Mills, South Wigston, *c.* 1898. The road to Countesthorpe crosses the former Leicestershire and Northamptonshire Union Canal in the background and the River Sence in the foreground. The canal was opened in 1792 and the canal company's cottage probably dates from that time. The windmill in the distance is on the land of Crow Mill Farm, while the water mill can be seen through the trees. Both mills were purchased by the canal company in 1818 for £900. The boys are standing on the bridle road to Blaby.

The wedding party of Sam Birkett, *c.* 1900. The group was photographed in the garden of 58 Blaby Road and the regal figure to the right of the front row is not who it appears to be!

SOUTH WIGSTON

Primitive Methodist

New School Chapel

Foundation

STONE LAYING

Ceremony,

SATURDAY, November 4th, 1899.

AT 2.45 P.M.

T. LAWRENCE, Esq., will deliver the ADDRESS.

The following Persons have kindly consented to Lay Stones:

Miss Annie Gamble, Master Harry Cecil Bates, W. T. Wright, Esq. (of Sileby), **Mr. C. Davis** (on behalf of Trustees) **Mr. W Franklin and others.**

A number of BRICKS, from 5 - and upwards will also be laid.

TEA WILL BE PROVIDED from 4-30 to 5-30 in the Wesleyan Schoolroom

NINEPENCE EACH. (Kindly Lent).

PUBLIC MEETING

At 6.45, in the Wesleyan Schoolroom.

Chairman	- -	MR. H. BATES.
Vice-Chairman	- -	MR. T. INGHAM.

Speakers: Revs. A. J. Smith, A. Walliker, T. Baron, I. J. Hardy, W. T. Wright, Esq. (of Sileby), and others.

SPECIAL SINGING by the COUNTESTHORPE CHOIR.

The Wesleyan Temperance BRASS BAND will also render Musical Selections on the Site and during the Meeting

Collection on the Site and at the Public Meeting in aid of Building Fund.

T. INGHAM, Printer, 20, Halford Street, Leicester.

The Primitive Methodist Chapel in Countesthorpe Road was opened in 1900 and merged with the Blaby Road Methodist church in 1967. The building was demolished in the 1980s and the site is now Best Close.

Above: The Windmill at Crow Mill Farm, c. 1900. This is the type known as a post mill, the structure is centrally pivoted and by means of the long curved pole above the ladder it can be turned to face the prevailing wind. The mill was demolished in the early years of the twentieth century.

Left: Queen Victoria's Diamond Jubilee Celebrations, 1897. To celebrate the occasion a drinking fountain was installed at the Bank in Wigston Magna and Mr Wignall is addressing the crowd.

Two

Edwardian Days

Leicester Road, c. 1906. This area between Bell Street and Aylestone Lane was formerly known as Balle Dyke. The signpost points to Bell Street while the shops beyond are still standing. The doorway in the left foreground leads to Forryan's Orchard while on the right is Peabody's jewellery shop, now the site of Wilkinson's store.

Wigston Magna from Welford Road, *c.* 1903. In front of All Saints church the former Asylum can be seen, while to the right of the picture is a new row of houses in Moat Street. These later became known as Peacock Row, apparently because one of the residents kept a peacock. The line of hedgerow and trees across the field in the foreground marks the course of Horsewell Lane, which was soon to have houses built along this section.

Blaby Road, *c.* 1904. Canal Street is to the left with Station Street in the bottom right-hand corner. The ivy-covered house beyond the row of shops is Ashbourne House, home of Orson Wright the 'father' of South Wigston. How peaceful our streets were on a sunny Edwardian afternoon.

Saffron Road, *c.* 1906. Behind the hedge on the left lies the Wigston Junction Brickworks from where much of the building material for South Wigston's houses was obtained. The horse-drawn van is approaching Toon and Black's Shoe Factory, while beyond lie Flude's Cottages on the corner of Kirkdale Road. These were among the first houses built in South Wigston.

Long Street, *c.* 1908. In the right foreground is the butcher's shop of Mr Freckingham. This was designed for that purpose and had a slaughterhouse at the rear. The two figures are standing on the corner of Central Avenue by the wall of Avenue House, while the farm buildings on the next corner are soon to be cleared for the new Co-operative Society building. In the distance the sign for the Durham Ox public house can be seen . The left foreground shows the railings of the National School and the prominent roof belongs to the Great Wigston Working Man's Club, opened in 1862 and reputedly the second oldest in the country. It continues to this day.

The wedding of George Jordan and Jane Kind, 1910. They were married at the Blaby Road Wesleyan chapel and were presumably photographed nearby although the exact location remains a tantalising mystery.

Two Steeples Cricket Club, 1907. The Two Steeples Company had its sports ground on Aylestone Lane where Northfield Avenue now stands.

'Ticker' Payne outside his shop at 58 Blaby Road,
c. 1908. One of South Wigston's more flamboyant
shopkeepers, he is remembered for owning one of
the town's first motor cars, a Model-T Ford. The
advertisement below dates from the same period.

25

Wigston railwaymen, c. 1902. The young lady is Ethel Howe, daughter of the Wigston stationmaster. The location of the photograph is difficult to pinpoint although the Midland 0-6-0 No.655 was a Wigston locomotive for many years.

Goods, guards and shunters in the Wigston Railway Yards, 26 December 1902. No railway shutdown over Christmas in those days! The impact of the railway on Wigston cannot be overestimated. The convergance of three routes, each with its own station and the building of engine sheds and marshalling yards in the 1870s required the employment of hundreds of men. Many came from other parts of the country to live here and the demand for housing was instrumental in the decision to begin construction of South Wigston in 1882.

Glen Parva Barracks, *c.* 1908. The barracks were built between 1877 and 1880 and became the headquarters of the Leicestershire Regiment. They served through both world wars and were gradually run down from the 1960s. Today only two of the original buildings remain.

Civilian Staff at Glen Parva Barracks, *c.* 1910.

The Opening Ceremony of St Mary's Catholic Church, South Wigston on 6 July 1905. The ceremony was performed by the Bishop of Nottingham. This church in Countesthorpe Road was the last of the major denominations in South Wigston to have its own building, which remains in use today. Prior to this date the chapel in the barracks had been used by the Catholic community.

A class from Great Wigston Council School, c. 1907. The headmaster on the left is Mr Thompson, with Miss Tarry the teacher on the right. Following the abolition of the school boards in 1903 responsibility for education was assumed by the local council. However, the pupils were colloquially known as 'Boardies' for many years afterwards. The former Board School has now been superbly restored and serves as the Leicestershire County Record Office.

The shop on the corner of Countesthorpe Road and Bassett Street, *c.* 1910. This shop was later taken over by Eric Holmes and became a bicycle shop (see page 103). The family now have their business along this entire block to the main shop on the corner of Blaby Road, with the centre building serving as the workshop. Apart from new plate-glass windows the scene remains substantially the same today.

Mrs Powell and her tearoom on Bull Head Street. This was built on to the front of the house and was situated just below the Queen's Head Hotel. For many years it sported a large cut-out teapot on the roof. Today the site is occupied by a filling station.

Leicester Road, c. 1905. On the left is the corner Aylestone Lane with Frederick Street going off to the right. The corner shop was the first in Wigston to sell frozen meat although for some time there was a reticence by most shoppers to buy this 'unnatural' product. All of these buildings have been swept away and replaced by purpose-built modern shops.

Bushloe End, c. 1910. The low building on the right was once the site of a framework knitting workshop and was later to become the Gas Board showrooms. Although some of the houses on the left remain, this scene is greatly changed today. The buildings on the right have all disappeared and Launceston Road gives access to the Little Hill Estate where the two boys are leaning on the wall.

Blaby Road, *c.* 1910. The shop with the awning on the left is Holmes' chemist, whose advertisement appears on the right. The two gentlemen to the right of the photograph are standing outside the bicycle shop of H. Smith on the corner of Countesthorpe Road. Bicycles are still sold here today by descendants of Eric Holmes, who took over the shop from Mr Pretty (who sold bicycles). How many Wigstonians first gained mobility on this corner?

ARTIFICIAL TEETH,

Complete Set,
Upper or
Lower
from £1 1s.

Single Tooth
from 2/6.
Perfect Fit Guaranteed.
EASY PAYMENTS.

REPAIRS, Etc. **Done on the shortest notice at Moderate Prices.**

Teeth Carefully Extracted 6d.

❧ Painless Extractions from 1/- ❧

MR. A. W. HOLMES

Has had 10 Years' Practical Experience.

☞ CONSULTATIONS AND ADVICE FREE.

Daily 8 a.m. to 8 p.m.   Tuesdays 8 a.m. to 2 p.m

Patients attended at their own homes for Extractions, etc., etc.,
on receipt of Post Card.

☜ DISTANCE NO OBJECT.

DRUGS, CHEMICALS, PHOTOGRAPHIC, INVALID & TOILET REQUISITES AT LEICESTER STORE PRICES.

ALL ORDERS PROMPTLY ATTENDED TO.

Note
the
Address **Wigston Drug Stores,**

CLIFFORD ST. & BLABY RD.,

SOUTH WIGSTON.

Wigston South Station, *c.* 1905. The train to Leicester is just arriving and the waiting passengers will be in the city within ten minutes.

Wigston South Station looking in the opposite direction to the picture above. The platforms here were staggered on either side of the Blaby Road level crossing. This was the first railway line through Wigston, opened by the Midland Counties Railway in 1840 as their main line to Rugby where connection was made with the London and Birmingham Railway. The first building behind the footbridge incorporated the original Wigston station building as its ground floor and housed the booking office. To the right of the footbridge the goods shed can be seen, while the smoking chimney shows that Bates' factory in Station Street was in full production. This line was merged into the Midland Railway in 1844 and remained as Wigston's access to London until 1857 when the Leicester to Hitchin line was opened (see page 12). With the opening of the station on that line this station became Wigston South. It was closed at the beginning of 1962 and the tracks were lifted a few years later. The site is now occupied by a health centre and the flats in Bennetts Way.

The level crossing at South Wigston, *c.* 1903. Between the trees the newly-built second Wigston station can be seen with the slope up to the new railway bridge over the main London railway line.

Wigston South Signal Box, *c.* 1905. Through the right-hand windows the large wheel which operated the level crossing gates can be seen. The field beyond the road belonged to Crow Mill Farm, by now usually known as Thornton's Farm. It was purchased by the Wigston Council in 1929 and became a public park, which it still is today.

Glen Parva Station, c. 1900. This was the third station to open in Wigston. Although the London and North Western Railway line from Nuneaton to Leicester had opened in 1864, this station was not built until 1884, no doubt with an eye on the new township of South Wigston then under construction. Midland Railway trains could also be seen passing through on their way to Birmingham although they did not call at the intermediate stations of the L.N.W.R.

The signal box on the platform of Glen Parva Station, c. 1900. The timber building behind is the station's booking office, with a ramp down to the platform. Passengers bound for the Nuneaton direction would have to cross the Saffron Road bridge to gain access to the other platform. Both photographs on this page are courtesy of the Leicestershire Record Office.

South Wigston's Iron Church with its successor behind. From 1886 to 1893 this building of corrugated iron served as the new township's Anglican church. Its official status was that of a Mission church in the parish of Great Wigston and only baptisms could be solemnised therein; the first was that of Albert Page on 8 May 1887. By the time the new brick church of St Thomas was consecrated in 1893, a total of 340 baptisms had taken place in the 'tin hut'. The new church was the centre of a new parish of Glen Parva and South Wigston. As well as baptisms, marriages could be performed there and the first was that of Joseph Gadsby and Ada Hennington on 18 September 1893. The Mission church had originally been under the jurisdiction of a curate- in-charge, the Revd G. Hamilton-Fraser. The first vicar appointed was the Revd W.G. Whittingham in 1891 and he continued in that post when the new church opened.

All Saints Church, Wigston Magna, c. 1902. This magnificent building stands on a corner of Wigston's original square of four roads and a church has been on this site for over a thousand years. Wigston's second church (see page 62) stood on the diagonally opposite corner and it is believed that they were originally the centres of two adjacent communities of Saxons and Danes respectively. The wall in the foreground is that of Rectory Farm, demolished in the 1920s. A staircase from the farmhouse can be seen today at Donington-le-Heath Manor house near Coalville.

Employees of Cook and Hurst's Hosiery Company, c. 1910. They are pictured outside the house where the firm began in business. This was the former home of the Lucas family and was located behind the corner of Long Street and Central Avenue.

Wigston Fire Brigade, c. 1907. They are pictured outside the fire station in Station Street, South Wigston. The fire engine's horses were kept in the field where Blaby Road Park is now located and on receiving an emergency call a fireman would be despatched to round up the horse. The brigade held monthly parades and would test their water jets by the canal at Crow Mills.

The Durham Ox Inn, c. 1904. Job Clark was the landlord and stands proudly before his door. This was one of Wigston's oldest hostelries and had previously been named the Woolsack and the Ram's Head. The brick section on the left was originally half-timbered and dates from the eighteenth century. The thatched part of the building is at least a hundred years older. The building was in Long Street by Blunts Lane.

The wedding party of John Thornton and Susan Ellen Brown, c. 1910. The Thornton family owned Crow Mill Farm and this group are posed in front of the farmhouse.

Left: Wigston Co-operative Society No.1 Branch, *c.* 1902. The society's headquarters was in Bell Street and this store was located in Moat Street on the corner of Cedar Avenue.

Below: Co-operative Butchers Department, *c.* 1902. Situated in Long Street opposite Central Avenue, the upper floor was tenanted by a local Friendly Society. Modern ideas on food hygiene were non-existent 90 years ago!

Above: The Duke of Clarence Hotel, *c.* 1903.
Situated in Blaby Road, this was very much the
centre of South Wigston's social life for the first 50
years of the new township. Also accommodating
the Clarence Assembly Rooms, most major civic
functions were held here as were dances and film
shows. In a later guise as the Gaiety one of the
rooms was named after Gertie Gitana, a famous
singer of the early years of the twentieth century. She
married Don Ross of Wigston and retained links
with the town until her death in 1957. Her grave is
in Wigston cemetery.

Right: Hardy's Grocery Shop, *c.* 1910. In Long Street,
the site is now the car park of the Conservative
Club. Dick Hardy liked to style himself as a 'high
class grocer'.

Above: Civic procession in Central Avenue. The occasion is not known but is possibly the coronation of Edward VII in 1902. Beyond the row of houses lie open fields and the cottage behind the horse brake was later pulled down to provide the site for the Co-operative garage.

Left: Wigston Foundry worker, *c.* 1903. The Wigston Foundry was established in Canal Street with the beginning of South Wigston in the early 1880s. The company had moved from Rotherham in Yorkshire and many of the workers came to Wigston from there. Its products can still be seen in some of the local streets.

Bassett Street School, c. 1904. The building behind the children became the girls' school, the boys' school was across the road while the infants' school was off the picture to the left. This building is the only one now remaining, having been beautifully restored as the South Wigston Community Centre.

Mr R. Kind and his Sunday School class, c. 1910. Mr Kind was a stalwart of the South Wigston Wesleyan chapel and had a haberdashery in Blaby Road.

Welford Road, c. 1906. The horse and trap have just crossed the junction of Moat Street and Newton Lane, with Bull Head Street behind them. The gentlemen on the left are probably watching a football match on the playing field off Horsewell Lane.

Cross Street Primitive Methodist Chapel, c. 1902. The building to the left of the chapel was once the farmhouse of the Wyggeston Hospital and both buildings are now incorporated into today's church.

AN OLD COTTAGE WIGSTON MAGNA. Nᵣ LEICESTER.

Above: Mr and Mrs Findlay's Cottage, *c.*
1907. This was at 78 Bull Head Street and
Mr Findlay was a thatcher by trade. The
cottage was demolished soon after the
Great War.

Right: Long Street, *c.* 1909. The row of
terraced houses are still there today apart
from the two at the far end which were
pulled down in the 1960s for a road-
widening scheme. The unusual three storey
house has also gone, replaced by a shop. A
tranquil scene so typical of the era.

Above: Leicester Road, *c.* 1904. Groups of children feature in so many early street scenes, but this one surpasses most! No doubt a photographer was then still a novelty. This was taken just past the corner of Burgess Street and the Star and Garter public house lies behind the house on the left.

Left: Dennis Dougherty and Norah Fitchett at the gate of 16 Clifford Street. The plate on the railings bears the name of Dr Briggs, a blind doctor from Wigston Magna who would come to South Wigston on one day of each week and hold a surgery in this house. He was a well-loved local figure, usually accompanied by an assistant who would describe visible symptoms of his patients. Local children knew him as a source of sweets, freely offered to anyone who would greet him in the street.

Crow Mill, *c.* 1903. Mr Redhead the miller stands proudly in front of his domain while a fisherman tries his luck on the opposite bank of the River Sence. A water mill has been recorded on this site since the thirteenth century, although by this time the mill could be driven by water or steam. Note the boiler house and chimney on the front. On the left the road to Countesthorpe crossing the bridge over the canal can be seen.

Crow Mills Viaduct, *c.* 1903. Although of poor quality, this is the only known photograph of the wooden trestle in use. A similar bridge once existed over the canal but was replaced by the steel bridge seen below the last carriage. Both viaducts have collapsed in the past, on one occasion the local miller prevented a disaster by stopping a train in time. This structure was replaced in 1912 (see page 53) and at the same time the brick arches were replaced by an earth embankment. The train is a Leicester to Rugby local.

The Old Noted Shop.

ESTABLISHED 1899.

F.W. COOPER

— PRACTICAL —

BOOT AND SHOE MAKER,

CLOSED UPPER, LEATHER AND
GRINDERY DEALER,

Canal St., South Wigston.

BOOTS & SHOES for EVERYBODY

Bespoke Orders and

REPAIRS

on the shortest notice.

A LARGE VARIETY OF BOOTS
AND SHOES ALWAYS IN . .
STOCK. . . . .

Hand-Sewn a Speciality

☞ Our Own Made Boots we guarantee.

GIVE THEM A TRIAL.

Above: Bell Street, *c.* 1910. A scene vastly different today, although the shops at the bottom in Leicester Road remain. Duncan Lucas, one of this book's authors, was born in the houses on the right beyond Hurst's builders yard.

Left: A 1909 advertisement for a shopkeeper popularly known as 'Cherry' Cooper.

46

World Record Bell Ringers, 1904. With the building of the tower of St Thomas' church in 1900 came the installation of a set of eight bells, all provided by Thomas Ingram. The bells were cast by Taylors of Loughborough and the first peal was rung on 2 November 1901. The record peal was rung on 27 December 1904 when 17,104 changes of Double Norwich Court Bob Major took 10 hours 35 minutes, which at the time was the longest peal ever rung.

Clarkes Road, c. 1908. In the left foreground Joseph and Mary Rawson stand outside their house. At the end of the street the section of road rising to cross the new bridge over the railway can be seen. The original road over the level crossing was in front of the white fence.

The Bank, *c.* 1907. The cottage on the left was the last thatched house in Wigston and was pulled down in the late 1940s. Behind the tree is the Queens Head public house and behind the carrier's cart is the fish, rabbit and poultry market. A market has been held on this site since at least the Civil War. Most old pictures of the Bank show vehicles gathered around the fountain and horse trough, and Wigston's early bus service to Leicester would also leave from here.

Oadby Lane, *c.* 1910. A baker's van stands outside St Wolstan's church.

Bull Head Street, *c.* 1904. The Georgian house at the top is on the Bank and the very narrow entrance to Oadby Lane goes off to the right. In the right foreground is the Traveller's Rest Inn, now the site of the Ladies Pride factory.

A military contingent in Blaby Road, 1909. The troops are marching towards Glen Parva Barracks led by a band, possibly having arrived at one of the Wigston stations. Leopold Street goes off to the left with the Duke of Clarence Hotel beyond. Note the people watching the parade on the balcony.

Bull Head Street, c. 1908. The gap in the row of houses on the left marks the site of the Horse and Trumpet public house, set back from the road. Behind the hedge on the right is Butts Close where archery practice was undertaken in medieval times. The police station now occupies this site.

Moat Street, c. 1903. The row of cottages on the left were always known as 'Diamond Cottages' from the shape of the window panes. Officially they were Midland and London Cottages. A framework knitting workshop stood in the yard behind.

Station Road, *c.* 1910. The cottages were known locally as 'Ten Row' and were pulled down around the end of the 1950s to make way for the College of Further Education. Abington House, home of Thomas Ingram, is off to the right of the photograph.

Harcourt Road, *c.* 1909. Although these houses are all still standing the shop front has now gone. A windmill once stood in the field to the right.

Left: Aftermath of a fire at Dunmore's Biscuit Factory in Canal Street 1903. This was one of Wigston's biggest fires to this date. Biscuits are still made on this site, lately under the Jacobs name.

Below: A leaflet published just after the fire to raise money for the many people thrown out of work.

THE DISTRESSING FIRE

AT THE BISCUIT WORKS OF
MESSRS. DUNMORE & SON, Ltd., SOUTH WIGSTON.

AN APPEAL TO THE GENERAL PUBLIC

☛ The proceeds of the sale of these to be divided amongst the distressed.

Kind friends of South Wigston and district,
  I hope you will read these few lines
Of the distressing fire we had here,
  And no doubt will cause some hard times .
For this could not have happened much worse,
  At this very bad time of the year,
And many a home will be wanting,
  And some will go hungry, I fear.

But we must not look on the dark side,
  For something will surely be done
To help those which are affected,
  And also the children at home.
For this is a case which is needy,
  And should receive the co-operation of all.
South Wigston friends, and district !
  For your kind support I now call.

We were always ready to help others
  In times that have gone by ;
And now to do your best for us,
  I hope each one will try.
In some cases it will come hard,
  Where families have to live ;
And those who can give them help,
  I hope will freely give.

Some years ago, you'll remember,
  When the bricklaying trade was bad,
And it was a very hard winter,
  For the men no work could be had –
But then some kind friend came forward,
  Now tell me who, if you can ;
Well, if you would like to know it,
  Mr. Dunmore was the man.

At his works in South Wigston, were made
  Some hundreds of loaves of bread,
Which were sent to the homes of the hungry
  Who were sadly in want, he said.
Don't you think that was a great kindness,
  To think of them in that way ?
It would comfort the homes of many,
  And give them meals for the day.

For his "hands" now I think you'll consider
  And you can help just a few
By purchasing one of these leaflets.
  When you have read this through.
As I draw these few lines to a close,
  I am sure that you can help many,
By taking one of these papers,
  The price of which is one penny.

Three

From 1911–1920

Crow Mills Viaduct, 2 September 1912. Workmen are gathered in preparation for the demolition of this wooden structure and its replacement by a steel and brick bridge (see also page 45).

Long Street, c. 1914. The Co-operative Society building on the corner of Central Avenue was built in 1910 and the first floor was used as a dancehall and meeting room. In the right foreground is the end of the wall of Wigston Hall. This corner of the hall's grounds was purchased by the post office in the 1950s to become the site of Wigston's main post office. It is now used solely as a sorting office.

Aylestone Lane, c. 1912. All of the houses on the left are still standing while the trees on the right have been replaced by the Curtis Weston Home, Kings Drive and the inevitable car park. Aylestone Lane was one of the principal roads into Medieval Wigston, and coal from the Leicestershire Coalfield would have arrived along this route by horse and pannier.

Moat Street, *c.* 1911. On the left is the sign of the Crown Inn while beyond is a well-known Wigston landmark, the cedar tree. Legend has it that this was one of three cedars planted in Wigston to commemorate the three Wigston soldiers who died in the Battle of Alma in 1856 during the Crimean War. It appears in many old photographs and its height is a useful dating guide. Most of the cottages on the right are still in existence. Note the slope of the road up to the kerb, this was later cut away to form a second kerb and undoubtedly caused some nasty falls in the wartime blackout.

Bushloe End, *c.* 1920. All of the buildings on the right have now gone, so have the houses beyond the shop on the left.

Frederick Street Factory Workforce, *c.* 1912. This building, the hosiery factory of A.E. Hill Limited, was on the site of the village hall. The railings of Bell Street Infants' school playground can be seen beyond.

South Wigston Adult School group, *c.* 1915. At this time the school occupied a corrugated iron hut in Bassett Street, a building later rebuilt in brick and now incorporated into a factory.

South Wigston Primitive Methodist Church football team of the 1912-13 season.

Wigston All Saints Church football team, 1911-12 season.

Saffron Road, *c.* 1915. The railings on the right were the beginning of the bridge over the railway line. Marstown Avenue goes off to the right and fields border Saffron Road beyond.

Kilby Bridge, *c.* 1912. This hamlet sprang up in the 1790s when the Leicestershire and Northamptonshire Union Canal reached this point on the Welford Road. On the right the Navigation Inn can be seen and Ellis' Yard is beyond. Another inn, the Black Swan, once stood on the opposite side of the road. It is recorded that in 1795 William Bellamy was appointed wharfinger at Kilby Bridge at ten shillings a week. In the 1880s the residents of Kilby Bridge formed a parish of East Wigston after a dispute with Wigston council over rates.

Blaby Road, c. 1911. On the right is the No.2 branch of the Wigston Co-operative Society. The modern 'Co-op' still occupies the site. Most of the houses beyond have now been converted into shops.

Countesthorpe Road, c. 1912. In the right foreground is the corner of Canal Street, while Countesthorpe Road turns right just beyond the trees. The houses past this corner are in Railway Street, with Water Street (now Park Road) at the end. The rear gardens of the latter ran down to the canal.

G. H. HUDDLESTON.

SPECIAL
FORD
AGENT.

Ford
THE UNIVERSAL CAR

SPECIAL
FORD
AGENT.

Measure their quality by the number on the road. A man of moderate means will want better value than a rich man—a greater interest on his investment. He can't afford to take chances. That is why he buys the Ford.

If it's hill climbing, ease of control, quiet running, comfort and economy, the Ford alone fills the bill. It answers every healthy purpose of road transport as efficiently as any automobile can. That is established. Now consider prices.

Runabouts £115

Five-passenger
Touring Car
£125

Town Car £175

Complete with full equipment, head lamps, side and tail lamps, horn, hood, windscreen, tyre pump, repair outfit, two boxes, tools and jack.

The Business Man's best means of conveying goods.

CHEAPER
THAN
HORSE
FLESH.

£150.

QUICKER
THAN
TRAINS.

With Canvas Top
£115

If you are interested in motor conveyances we shall be pleased to give you practical demonstrations of the car or van, and are prepared to keep same in running order, including tyres, petrol, oil, etc., for 3d. per mile.

GARAGE AND WORKS:

Blaby Road, South Wigston.

Telephone 83 Wigston.

Above: The Royal Oak, 1911. Mr Thorpe the landlord and his wife prepare to set off in their pony trap. At this time there were few houses in this section of Leicester Road, the area later became known as Wigston Fields. Photograph courtesy of the Leicestershire Record Office.

Left: An advertisement for Huddleston's Garage, 1915. See page 103.

Coronation Day Procession, 1911. A Boy Scout contingent leads the parade along Clifford Street in South Wigston.

Coronation Day Street Party, 1911. Just around the corner from the previous photograph, civic dignitaries sit at tables in the middle of Blaby Road. Note the fields beyond the Saffron Road corner and the old iron church to the right, this was now used as schoolrooms by St Thomas' church.

Above: South Wigston Wesleyan Chapel, c. 1914. This was the frontage of the 1902 rebuilding, with two side doors beside the main entrance. The iron railings disappeared for use as scrap metal during wartime.

Left: St Wolstan's Church, c. 1920. Over the years this church has been named both St Wolstan's and St Wistan's. St Wistan was a local Saxon prince murdered at nearby Wistow, while St Wolstan is believed to have been a twelfth century Bishop of Worcester. It is reputed to be the only church in the country to bear either name. The blank north wall shown here now has two windows and before 1600 an aisle was attached to the church at this point. The tower is thirteenth century, the chancel nineteenth century.

Right: St Thomas' Church, *c.* 1912. The view is from the vicarage garden, with part of the vicarage visible on the right. The church tower had a clockface added to three sides in 1919 as part of South Wigston's tribute to its fallen sons of the Great War.

Below: Cross Street Methodist Chapel, *c.* 1920. Beyond the Welford Road corner Newton Lane has only a few houses before the open fields. The last building in the row was a framework knitting workshop.

Welford Road, c. 1911. The signpost points to Newton Lane and Moat Street. For many years this part of Welford Road was known as Wharf Road as it led to the canal wharf at Kilby Bridge. The hill itself was called Gilliver Hill. Before the coming of the railways much of Wigston's coal and building materials would have come down this hill and perhaps some of the town's products were taken away by canal.

Saffron Road, c. 1920. Toon and Black's Shoe Factory dominates this section of the road and was a major employer in South Wigston for many years and was finally demolished in the 1980s. Jasmine Court now occupies the site. The factory extends as far as Kirkdale Road.

Blaby Road, c. 1912. Ashbourne House is the residence built by Orson Wright in the heart of the new settlement he had created. Following his death in 1913 the house was occupied by a succession of doctors, serving also as their surgery. It was finally pulled down in 1962, to be replaced by a nondescript row of shops. The next large house over Albion Street is the Limes, the home of Mr Gamble the shoe manufacturer. It serves today as the South Wigston Conservative Club.

Long Street, c. 1912. The gentleman with the bicycle is standing at the gate of the Hall. On the left is the Congregational chapel, built in 1841, beyond is the Manse. The wall on the left is now the site of the Peace Memorial Park, created after the First World War. At the time of this photograph it was a paddock where the Hall's horses would graze.

New recruits at Glen Parva Barracks, 1914.

Soldiers at Glen Parva, c. 1915. From their cap badges they appear to be of the Leicestershire Regiment. Other troops look on from the balcony behind. How many of them returned?

Soldiers from Glen Parva convalescing, c. 1916. They are posed around what appears to be a Model-T Ford belonging to the ABC Carrier Company. Behind them is the corner of Blaby Lane and Saffron Road, later to be the depot of ABC.

Swain Family Group, c. 1915. The Swains were connected with the Wigston Foundry and the soldier (James Smith) joined the 164 (Rotherham) Brigade of the Royal Artillery. The other people are George Swain, Horace Swain, Hilda Swain and the two children of Mabel Swain.

'Royal Party L.R.I.' This is the inscription on the back of the original postcard, but it is believed to have been taken for the 1911 coronation celebrations. The passengers in the carriage have been identified as Mr and Mrs Charles Holt, Lily Wait and Bessie Hodgkin who was the sister of Thomas Goodin, a manufacturer of soft drinks in Spa Lane. The picture was taken on the corner of Mowsley End and Bull Head Street.

The Congregational Chapel in Blaby Road, c. 1914. Built in 1896, it still serves today. On the right the Limes and its large greenhouse can be seen.

Moat Street, c. 1911. Once again the cedar tree is prominent and on the left is the No. 1 branch of the Co-operative Society. The two boys with the barrow are probably collecting horse manure, a lucrative source of pocket money in those days.

Empire Day, c. 1916. This was celebrated on Queen Victoria's birthday, 24 May. Duncan Lucas' mother, Margaret Forryan, is the second from the left in the back row.

The Royal Train passing through Wigston, 1914. Wigston's marshalling yard can be seen above the coaches, while the buildings in the background are the engine sheds and wagon repair shops. The house directly above the locomotive was the stationmaster's residence. The occupants of Midland Cottages are at their doors to see their monarch pass. This photograph was taken from the bridge on Blaby Road and the scene remained substantially the same until the 1970s.

All Saints Church from the south. This unusual view was probably taken from the top of the retort house at the gasworks. Yew Tree Farm is in the foreground with the farmhouse beyond the barn. The manor house is in front of the church and Gas Lane crosses the left foreground.

Leicester Road, *c.* 1914. This view is looking towards the centre of Wigston and of all the buildings seen here, only the Star and Garter on the right remains.

Leicester Road and Long Street, *c.* 1919. The wall on the left belongs to Forryan's Farm, with the orchard behind it. The road in this area was built over running sand and frequently collapsed.

Left: Glen Parva Grange Lodge, *c.* 1912. Although the Grange was pulled down many years ago, both lodges still serve as residences. This wintry scene is believed to be the Top Lodge.

Below: Victory Tea, 1919. Held in the girls' school in Bassett Street, this main hall remains as part of the new community centre.

Top Lodge, Saffron Road, c. 1916.

Welford Road at Kilby Bridge, c. 1913. The bridge in the foreground is over the River Sence and the original humpback bridge over the canal can be seen just in front of the buildings. The canal bridge was replaced with a wider structure in 1937 with the upgrading of the road which is now the A50 trunk road.

Left: Workers at Dent's prefabricated building works in Leicester Road, 1916.

Below: The original Little Hill, c. 1910. These cottages were behind Cross Street and the name is perpetuated in the large housing estate on the other side of Moat Street.

Four

The 1920s

Huddleston's Garage and Shop, Blaby Road, c. 1927. This enterprising family concern began here in the early years of the twentieth century and occupied the site for over sixty years. They began by selling prams and bicycles, which were at one time their own make. By 1915 they were agents for Ford motor cars (see page 60) and for some years owned the Midland Cafe across the road. It is said that the mechanics would ring a bell when they wanted a cup of tea and it would be brought across the road!

Above: Wigston Station, c. 1921. This was the 'new' station on the main line, opened in 1902 with the building of the road bridge seen above the train. It was renamed Wigston Magna by the London Midland and Scottish Railway in 1924.

Left: Thornton's Farm, South Wigston, c. 1929. Sheep are being loaded into the van of Rawlinson's family butchers (see page 126). Above the van is the concrete base of the old windmill shown on page 20, while beyond is the railway embankment and the Wigston Foundry chimney.

Wigston Laundry, *c.* 1925. This was an advertising postcard which customers could send in with a date and time at which they would like their laundry to be collected. This is now the site of the B & Q hardware store in Bull Head Street.

Transport transition, *c.* 1925. Drivers pose proudly in front of their Wigston Laundry vans, with a superseded horse van behind. The drivers are Mr Norman (left), Frank Upton and Reynold Stevens (centre) and Joe Carter by the horse. Local farmers would often buy superannuated vehicles from the laundry's fleet.

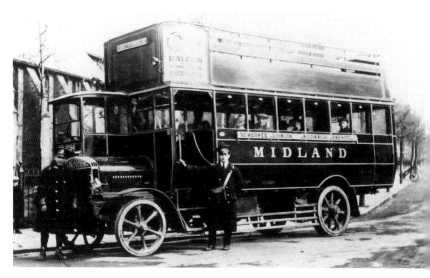

Above: Midland Red Omnibus, *c.* 1925. This venerable Tilling-Stevens open-top bus is standing in front of St Thomas' church. It was on the route from the Hind Hotel in Leicester to Wigston Magna, South Wigston and the Newarkes.

Left: Fitchett's shop in Blaby Road, *c.* 1924. Mrs Fitchett and her daughter Marjorie stand in the doorway.

Above: The funeral of Mrs Franklin, *c.* 1925. Mrs Franklin was the wife of a railwayman and lived in Midland Cottages. At the time of her death one of her sons lived in Canada and a photographer was engaged to record all stages of the funeral for the emigree. Here the hearse stands outside the Railway Hotel before beginning the climb up Station Road towards Wigston cemetery.

Right: 1908 advertisement. Although some seventeen years earlier, it is quite possible that the hearse depicted is the same shown in the photograph above.

T. H. Hodgkin,

Complete Funeral Furnisher.

9 & 11 Long Street, Wigston.

Artificial Wreaths and Crosses stocked.

Every description of Coffins made to order on the shortest notice at most reasonable terms.

☞ *Mourning Cards printed on the shortest notice.*

ALL ORDERS PROMPTLY ATTENDED TO UNDER THE PERSONAL SUPERVISION OF THE OWNER.

T. H. wishes to draw attention to his **Pair-Horse Saloon Brake**, movable top—latest design. Parties accommodated attending Opera, Dances, etc.

Brougham and Landaus for Hire.

BEST TURNOUTS.   REASONABLE TERMS.

WHY GO TO LEICESTER?

The Wilfred Brothers, *c.* 1923. They were dairymen for the Wigston Co-operative Dairy which was in Bushloe End (see page 100). They are pictured here on the corner of Moat Street and Newgate End.

Harrison's delivery van, *c.* 1926. Harrison's Salt Works was in Canal Street and their 'Two Steeples' brand of table salt was a common feature of dinner tables for many years.

Constone Works, South Wigston, c. 1929. An advertising postcard showing the firm's yard and stockpile of concrete products. Much of this site is the old Wigston Junction Brickworks, by now no longer in production. The old brickyard chimney on the left was toppled around 1929-30.

Albert G. Shipp,

COAL MERCHANT,

Railway Station, Wigston.

LEICESTERSHIRE AND DERBYSHIRE HOUSE COALS.

Orders from Blaby, Whetstone, Countesthorpe and Oadby will receive prompt :: :: attention.

An advertisement from 1915. Shipp's coal yard was off Blaby Road, adjacent to South Wigston station.

Blaby Road, c. 1925. Taken from outside Ashbourne House on the corner of Glengate with the level crossing in the distance. At this time the Brittanic Assurance Company occupied the far corner of Canal Street.

Saffron Road, c. 1928.

Mr Alf Painter outside the Bull's Head Inn, c. 1929. Mr Painter was a fruiterer and a well-known figure around Wigston. The licensee of the Bull's Head at this time was Walter Privitt.

Old cottages in Butts Close. These cottages were once owned by the Wyggeston Hospital and were demolished in the 1960s. To the right is one of several mud walls still extant in Wigston at this time, dating back to medieval times. The new extension to the Wigston Laundry is taking shape in the middle distance.

Above: Civic dignitaries at the beginning of house building in Northfield Avenue, *c.* 1929. Those present include Bill Gunning, Canon Wright, Frank Woodward and Bronx Snowden.

Left: Holt's Grocers, Bushloe End. The building remains today as a guest house and traces of the painted brewery sign can still be discerned.

Mr Charles Moore and Miss Kathleen Veasey, *c.* 1929. 'Charlie' Moore was one of South Wigston's best-known figures for almost 50 years, not least for his position as conductor of the Wigston Temperance Band. His shop on the corner of Blaby Road and Canal Street was a mecca for music lovers.

Wendouree Dance Orchestra, *c.* 1925. The leader (centre) was Mr W.G. Hall, proprietor of a photographic business in Blaby Road. Mr Beardman is on the left with Joe Green and Sid Partridge behind.

Heatherly House. Off Station Road, its grounds adjoined those of Bushloe House (page 95). Part of the site is now the Wigston College of Further Education.

The extensive greenhouses at Heatherley House.

Above: The Picture House in Blaby Road, 21 April 1930. Patrons are queueing for the film *Under The Greenwood Tree,* the first 'talkie' to be shown in South Wigston. The cinema was owned by George Smith and opened in 1920, although films had earlier been shown at the Duke of Clarence Hotel across the road. This building received a new façade in 1938 and was renamed the Ritz. Its last film was shown in 1980 and it is now known as Ritz Bingo.

The PICTURE HOUSE
BLABY ROAD.   SOUTH WIGSTON.

Proprietor and Manager :   GEORGE SMITH.

'Phone 85 WIGSTON.

ONE PERFORMANCE NIGHTLY
DOORS OPEN AT 7.   COMMENCE AT 7.30.
SATURDAY, Two Performances, 6.0 & 8.0.
DOORS OPEN 5.30.

MATINEE on Saturday for Children
Doors Open 1.30.   Commence at 2.   Admission 2d.   Back Seats 3d.

Prices of Admission : 5d., 8d., 1/-, 1/3.

No Half-Price Tickets Saturdays and Holiday Weeks.

SPECIAL NOTICE
The Picture House Orchestra now augmented under the
Directorship of Mr. R. E. DODSLEY, renders
First Class Music each evening.

Wigston Council School Football Team, 1924-25 season.

South Wigston Boy Scouts, 1928.

The wedding of Orson Lucas and Margaret Forryan, 1923.

Children of the National School, c. 1928. The group appear to be ready for a procession, most likely to a service at All Saints church.

Frederick Street, c. 1925. The Wesleyan Methodist chapel on the left at the far end of the street is the only building shown here which is still standing.

Newgate End, c. 1923. The building on the right is the former Asylum House, while to the extreme left is Squire Knob's farmhouse, at this time the home of Arnold Forryan.

St Wolstan's House, Oadby Lane, *c.* 1926. Originally a farmhouse known as Hungerton House, it stands across Church Nook from St Wolstan's church and bore its present name by 1892. Built around 1856 it was the home of the Eggleston and Morley families for almost a century. During the Second World War it served as an ARP centre and remains as a handsome private home today.

Station Road, *c.* 1927. The houses of Bushloe End appear in the distance and the grounds of Heatherly and Bushloe Houses are behind the trees on the left.

South Wigston Girls' School class, *c.* 1929.

Workers at J.G. Glover's Hosiery Factory, Canal Street, *c.* 1920. The central figure is George Findley.

A donkey cart at the rear of Glen Parva Grange, c. 1920. The young ladies in the cart are Clarice Clover and Dorothy Wright. Miss Wright's father, John, is holding the donkey.

Revd Colin Weston, c. 1922. The Revd Weston was the vicar of St Thomas' from 1916 to 1939, the longest serving incumbent in the parish. He is pictured here behind the vicarage.

Jordan's Charabancs, c. 1925. Mr Jordan ran a hire company and garage in Clifford Street throughout the 1920s.

Charles Moore's Corner, c. 1922. Jack Boulter the postman is handing a letter to Kathleen while Charles, Norah and Ted Moore are posed around the building. The end of Deeming Brothers' Printing Works can be seen in Canal Street.

Five

The 1930s

Bushloe House. Perhaps the largest private house in Wigston, it was built in 1850 by Stephen Fry, an architect and surveyor, as his own residence. It was purchased by Hiram Abiff Owston, a Leicester solicitor, in 1866 and substantial additions were made to the house in 1880. It remained in the Owston family until the 1940s when it was acquired by Wigston Urban District Council for use as its offices. With considerable modern extensions it serves today as the administration centre of Oadby and Wigston Borough Council.

The Bank and Bull Head Street, c. 1930. The imposing building in the centre was built as a British School for which pupils paid one or two old pence a week to attend. It later became a Mechanics' Institute. 'Chippy' Ray's Bank fish shop on the right was not pulled down until the 1980s. Apart from the Queen's Head on the left, all the buildings shown here have now gone, replaced by the new dual carriageway.

Blaby Road, c. 1935. Dunton Street is still cobbled while on the opposite corner stands a short-lived design of telephone kiosk.

Fairfield Street, South Wigston, *c*. 1930. On the left is the Duke of Clarence Hotel, with a sign in the yard still proclaiming 'Good Stabling with Loose Boxes To Let'. Further down the street are council houses, built in the 1920s. The South Wigston Post Office on the right corner was in the hands of W.A. Deeming whose postcards of local views appear many times in these pages.

Victoria Street, *c*. 1938. Viewed from Leicester Road, the timber building on the right was Clay's Garage, one of Wigston's first mechanical repair workshops and once a bicycle manufacturer. The building burnt down in the 1940s.

Magna Cinema

LONG STREET, WIGSTON MAGNA.
'Phone: Leicester 89526.

Grand OPENING
of LEICESTER'S ULTRA-MODERN CINEMA
BOXING DAY, DEC. 26th.

First House Commence 5-30 p.m.   Doors Open 5 p.m.
Second House Commence 8-30 p.m.

Special Screening of——

GRACIE

FIELDS

in her latest success—

SING AS WE GO

(Cert. "U")

With a FULL SUPPORTING PROGRAMME including:—
WALT DISNEY'S
SILLY SYMPHONY COLOURED CARTOON.

PRICES: 6d., 9d., 1/- and Balcony 1/3.

Thursday, Friday, Saturday——Continuous from 6 to 11 p.m.
SPECIAL MATINEES: Thursday & Friday at 2-30 p.m.
CHILDREN'S MATINEE SATURDAY, DEC. 27th at 2 p.m.
Admission: 2d.   Balcony: 3d.
FREE CAR PARK.   FREE CAR PARK.

Poster for the opening of the Magna Cinema in 1934.

Sunday School outing, *c.* 1934. Photographed from the Wigston Station offices, this happy group are possibly bound for Wicksteed Park at Kettering.

Methodist Sisterhood outing, *c.* 1930. The ladies are standing on the opposite platform to the group in the top photograph. Access to the platforms was through entrances in the parapet of the bridge and down covered staircases.

Wigston Co-operative Society Dairy, c. 1932. Situated in Bushloe End, the site is now Parlour Close. Much of the milk processed here came from local farmers.

Workers in Gamble's Shoe Factory, Canal Street, c. 1930.

Right: Wigston railwaymen, *c.* 1931. They are posed on a former Midland Compound 4-4-0 at the rear of the Wigston sheds. The tall gentleman second from right is Albert Franklin.

Below: Glen Parva Barracks main gate, *c.* 1935. The posters on the gate pillars are for the Leicestershire Regiment.

ENTRANCE, GLEN PARVA BARRACKS

Aerial view of Wigston Magna, c. 1930. In the foreground is the Congregational chapel, with the Memorial Park beyond. Across Long Street is Wigston Hall and the first rows of houses are in Paddock Street. Oadby Lane can be seen in the top right corner, Leicester Road goes off to the top left. Housing now covers virtually all the fields in the background.

Paddock Street, c. 1938. Then a dead-end street with the wall of Long Lane at the bottom, it has since been extended to Bull Head Street and now forms part of a busy through route.

Eric Holmes' first shop, c. 1934. On the corner of Countesthorpe Road and Bassett Street it is still in the hands of the Holmes family. See also page 29.

Huddleston's Garage, Blaby Road, c. 1933. George Huddleston, founder of the business in 1906, is on the left and his son Ralph stands beside him. The garage closed in the 1960s and the site is now a factory car park. See also page 75.

Civic procession on the occasion of the death of King George V, January 1936. Wigston Temperance Band lead, with an army contingent behind them. Then come representatives for the police force, civic officials and other groups including St John's ambulance brigade. The large building behind is on the corner of Station and Pullman Roads and was at this time the main offices of Wigston Council. It later served as the Wigston Police Station.

Orson Wright's Ladies Cricket Team, 1931. The name of South Wigston's founder was perpetuated at this time by a shoe factory in Canal Street.

Bassett Street Infants' School teaching staff, c. 1930. The headmistress, Miss Richardson, is in the centre of the group.

Wigston Conservative Club Glee Party, 1935.

MORRISON-ELECTRIC

THE URBAN TRANSPORT SYSTEM
OF THE
ELECTRIC AGE!

CHEAPER THAN THE HORSE—

QUICKER ON URBAN DELIVERY THAN THE
PETROL VAN

MORE HYGENIC THAN EITHER

A. E. MORRISON & SONS, LTD. SOUTH WIGSTON

Morrison Electric factory yard, c. 1937. This company moved to South Wigston from Leicester in 1934 and established their works in the former Brunswick Mills in Garden Street. They produced all types of electric vehicles and their products could be seen over much of the world. The company later merged with Crompton-Parkinson and moved to South Wales in the 1960s. See also page 127.

Wigston Gas Works, *c.* 1930. The Great Wigston Gaslight and Coke Company was formed in 1857 and the gas works were built at the end of Newgate End. The final section of the road was later renamed Gas Lane. The original limited company was incorporated by an Act of Parliament, 'The Great Wigston Gas Act' of 24 June 1889. The gas works closed in the 1950s.

Wigston Locomotive Depot, *c.* 1934. These sheds were opened in 1873 and coded 11 by the Midland Railway. In 1920, a total of 52 engines were allocated, mostly freight types. It closed on 5 November 1934 but was reinstated in 1945 to act as a sub-shed of Leicester during the latter's rebuilding. It finally went out of use in the mid 1950s. Note the reserve coal stack on the left.

Lewin family members, 7 June 1930. Bill, Ernie, Stella, Jess and Ern are in the rear garden of the family home at 20 Central Avenue. The authors are grateful to the late Stella Lewin for supplying a number of the photographs in this book.

Leicester Infirmary parade, 1937. The annual infirmary parades were a popular feature of both Wigston Magna and South Wigston during the years between the two world wars. Various organisations would vie to decorate the best float and the proceeds would provide beds (with a suitably inscribed plaque) in the Royal Infirmary. This was the float of the South Wigston Primitive Methodist chapel.

Armistice Day service, c. 1930. Wreaths are laid on the South Wigston war memorial in the grounds of St Thomas' church. Following the Second World War a second level was added to the memorial. The brick building behind the soldiers is the new church schoolrooms, completed in 1928 on the site of the old 'iron church'.

A peaceful moment in Blaby Road Park, c. 1935. The amenities building still exists today but the railway footbridge and platform behind have long since disappeared.

Above: Saffron Lane, *c.* 1930. A view from the parapet of the tower of St Thomas' church. To the left is the site of the brickworks and Glen Parva Station forms the far boundary. Beyond are the barracks.

Left: Moat Street, *c.* 1934. Another church tower view, this time from All Saints. In the distance houses have been built in Newton Lane to the top of the hill, compare with the view on page 63.

Wigston Hall. Another contender for the largest house in Wigston, it was located in Long Street on the land now occupied by Elizabeth Court. Built in 1834, in its later years it was the home of several schools and finally a fashion centre.

ABC Garage, c. 1937. The ABC Carrier Company was formed by Mr Kibble, a South Wigston fishmonger, about 1914 and was reputedly named after a teashop where he courted the lady who became his wife. The firm is still in business on the same site although now solely as a filling station and workshop.

Above: Wigston Temperance Band, 1935. Mr Charles Moore proudly leads the band along Blaby Road past Canal Street. This was the first outing of the band's new dark green uniforms, in honour of the silver jubilee of King George V.

Left: Jack Thornton thatching a haystack at Crow Mill Farm, *c.* 1930. The joining of the two ladders would cause a raised eyebrow in today's safety-conscious era!

Six

The 1940s

Wigston Station entrance, c. 1940. Teacher Stella Laundon and a special constable lead a party of boys over 'Spion Kop'. The brick archway led to the covered staircase down to the London-bound platform.

Left: Wigston's bomb. A lone German aircraft dropped three bombs over South Wigston in 1941. The first fell in the front garden of this house in Saffron Road while the other two exploded harmlessly in the fields behind. Legend has it that the pilot was aiming for a light incautiously showing at the Grange across the road.

Below: Victory Maypole, 1945. Margaret and Eileen Charles proudly pose in their Land Army uniforms before setting off with their band of happy children. The scene is the yard of Upper Farm which was behind the Chestnuts in Spa Lane.

Above: South Wigston Home Guard, *c.* 1945.

Right: Eddie Brandon on leave, *c.* 1944.
Mr Brandon's father was the signal man at South
Sidings box and during a visit to the workplace
Eddie poses nonchalantly with his foot on the down
main line.

Lansdowne Grove, c. 1948. This estate was built in the 1930s by a consortium headed by Ernest Hooley and was popularly known as Hooley's Estate. Many of the houses remained empty for some years until Wigston received evacuees from the London Blitz in 1940 when they were hurriedly pressed into service.

Leicester Road, c. 1945. The farm buildings of Forryan's Farm still occupy the corner of Bell Street although by now almost derelict. Note the white markings on the base of the lamp post on the left, a legacy of the years of the wartime blackout.

Above: Aerial view of Wigston, 1947. With the post-war demand for housing, Wigston Council began the construction of a large estate on the fields at the end of Central Avenue. Aylestone Lane crosses the back of this scene with Station Road to the front. In the foreground is Abington House, its surrounding fields are now occupied by Abington, Bushloe and Guthlaxton schools.

Right: Mrs H.G. Lucas casts her vote in the 1945 general election. This venerable old lady was grandmother to one of this book's authors.

117

Army Parade in South Wigston, 1948. Men of the Leicestershire Regiment are marching from Glen Parva Barracks to Wigston Magna station en route to a posting in Hong Kong.

South Wigston tennis players, c. 1947. Some of the local businessmen were wont to gather at the Barracks' tennis courts for a friendly game. They are, from left to right: Wilf Allsop, George Smith, -?-, Bill Eliot, Ernie Andrews, Percy Weston, Cec Eaton and Clem Bass.

Seven

The 1950s

South Wigston Old Boys Rugby Football Club. The team enjoyed particular success for some years from the late 1940s, culminating in the selection of Les Armson, Pat Hunt and David Hillsdon as Schoolboy Internationals in 1951. Here the team are about to commence their 1950 Easter Tour.

Bell Street Infants' School. Built in 1873 this was the first Wigston Board School after the passing of the 1870 Education Act and was a typical Victorian structure. A two-storey building was later added on the Frederick Street frontage. The whole site is now occupied by Sainsbury's supermarket.

Teaching staff of the Wigston Church of England Schools, c. 1957. By this period both the former Board and National schools had combined and pupils would usually attend two years at each. The teachers are, standing, from left to right: Mr Herrick (headmaster), Mr Tyler, Mr Widdowson, Miss Root, Mr Tuxford, Mr Crane, Mr Baxter. Seated: Miss Piston, Mrs Insley, Mrs Parker, Miss Hewes, Miss Daft, Miss Samson, Miss Rolland, Miss Marvin, Miss Allsop. Front: Mrs Harrison, Mr Harries.

Landsdowne Grove, South Wigston.

New Council Housing in Lansdowne Grove, *c.* 1955. The land for this estate had previously been a part of Crow Mills Farm and the council also established playing fields between the estate and the railway line.

Long Street, *c.* 1959. The junior school can be seen on the left (now the Leicestershire Record Office) while the shop in the right foreground was called the Joke Shop and proved very popular with the school's pupils!

South Wigston Evergreen Club, c. 1956.

A social tea in the Wigston Constitutional Hall, c. 1957. The Constitutional Hall in Cross Street was built in the early years of the twentieth century and was a popular venue for dances and other social events. It still stands today although no longer used for its original purpose.

St Thomas' Church Choir, c. 1952.

Mr and Mrs W.L. Freeman and Mr and Mrs C. Moore, c. 1958. Two well-known South Wigston business families who by this date could muster almost a century of service between them. Freeman's furniture shop finally ceased trading in 1994, C. Moore and Son's music shop in 1972.

Ashbourne House in Blaby Road, c. 1959. By this date the doctors surgery of Redmond and Yates. Its demolition in 1962 was a tragic loss to the South Wigston streetscape and a link with the town's founder.

Forryan's Gold Hill Stores, 1953. This was located on Aylestone Lane almost opposite what is now Shackerdale Road. At this time the shop was surrounded by fields and it took its name from one of the early three great fields of Wigston, the other two were Tythorn and Mucklow. The shop was decorated for the coronation. In medieval times Shackerdale meant Robber's Valley.

Eight

1960 Onwards

Final days of Blaby Road Level Crossing, 1965. Following the closure of the Leicester to Rugby line at the beginning of 1962, it had been used to store surplus wagons for several years. Here the final demolition train takes the track with it and soon the gates will open to road traffic for the last time in 125 years. Note the edge of Huddleston's Garage on the right and the magnificent iron footbridge.

Countesthorpe Road, c. 1967. This row of houses was one of the first built in South Wigston and was known as Apostle's Row, the houses were named after the Twelve Apostles. They were pulled down in the 1970s and replaced by flats and a car park. The house on the left was once the home of Mr Bates, for many years a local manufacturer and philanthropist.

Rawlinson's Grocery and Butchers Shop, c. 1960. On the corner of Countesthorpe and Blaby Roads, it was pulled down at the same time as the houses in the above photograph. The Rawlinson family owned two shops in Blaby Road, this one was run by Albert, while his brother Peter ran the shop on the corner of Dunton Street.

Morrison Electric, *c.* 1965. Mr Ernest Follows tests the latest vehicle produced at the Garden Street works. Completed chassis such as this were a common sight around the streets of South Wigston, being either on test or en route to a body works for completion.

The last one, 1968. By now under the name of Austin Crompton Parkinson Ltd, the former Morrison Electric factory turned out its last vehicle in 1968 before the move to new premises in Tredegar, South Wales. This final milk float was bound for Express Dairies and some of the longest serving craftsmen pose for their picture around it, each had signed his name upon the front.

Above: Long Street, c. 1970. In the left foreground is the Working Men's Club and further along the fondly-remembered Magna Cinema. Its latter days had been as a snooker club and it was finally demolished in 1992. The site is now a modern nursing home but the distinctive 1930s façade of the Magna has been skilfully incorporated into the entrance of its successor.

Left: A new era, 1981. Mrs Primrose Wray as mayor of Oadby and Wigston Borough Council raises the European Economic Community's flag in the grounds of Bushloe House, watched by a representative of Wigston's French twin town, Maromme, and former mayor, Mr Fred Bennett.